Intent and Innovation

Branding for the Modern Entrepreneur

Joaby-Wan

ISBN: 978-1-965703-00-7

First Edition

Visit us at www.nully.pro

Intent and Innovation

Intent and Innovation

To all the mistakes made along the way,
And to my muse,
For always improving my perspective and
defying my perception, pushing me to see the world
in ways I never imagined.

"We are all members."

— *F.G*

Contents

Intent

———◦❖❖❖◦———

Congratulations are well-deserved—not just for starting your own venture, but for having the courage to strive for excellence where many others simply maintain the status quo. Owning a business is not easy; it requires resilience and a continuous pursuit of improvement. If you're reading this, you're already on the right path, and I genuinely admire your boldness. Whether you've already started your business or are just considering it, I'm proud of you for taking this significant step.

As we explore the narratives in this book, understand that it's not just about business—it's about mastering the art of commerce, an ever-evolving practice from ancient bazaars to today's digital marketplaces. You have stepped into an arena where many have faltered, and for that, you deserve recognition. Be it the commerce of goods, emotions, or knowledge, the essence of trade remains a profound exchange that shapes our world.

Before we even begin to conceptualize what, a good business should look like or how it should operate, there are more important matters at hand. Throughout this book, we will delve into a multitude of ideas, methodologies, tips, tools, and perspectives on how people perceive businesses. However, one central theme will remain constant: intention.

Intention is the driving force behind every successful business, shaping its purpose, guiding its actions, and influencing its outcomes. If you take away anything from this book, let it be this fundamental principle.

But why is Intent so crucial? Because by understanding the intent, we uncover a whole new layer of knowledge. It connects dots across disciplines, making complex ideas surprisingly clear and approachable. It's like suddenly seeing the blueprint behind a complex machine. This understanding transforms how we think, enhancing our ability to question and to learn.

Imagine approaching every new piece of information with this mindset. What deeper truths could we uncover about the world and ourselves? By focusing on the Intent, we equip ourselves to think more critically, ask more insightful questions, and make more meaningful connections. It's not just about gathering facts; it's about grasping the very essence that stitches those facts together.

In a world where distractions are plentiful and focus is a fleeting commodity, it's easy to get lost in the haze of everyday life. We find ourselves perpetually torn, it's easy to get distracted by the noise and lose sight of what truly matters. Our minds are constantly bombarded with notifications, social media, and endless to-do lists, making it difficult to cultivate a sense of purpose and direction. But what if there was a way to cut through the clutter, to silence the din, and to tap into a deep sense of purpose and direction?

For centuries, the ancient Japanese art of Shodo, or calligraphy, has held the secrets of cultivating intent, discipline, and mindfulness. Each brushstroke in Shodo is executed with such expert intent that only other masters, possessing a high level of qualification and expertise, can fully appreciate the depth and meaning behind them. This level of mastery highlights the profound understanding and knowledge embedded within the art form. Unlike the common belief that art must convey specific emotions or narratives, Shodo emphasizes the purity of intention and the precision of execution, creating a meditative practice that transcends mere representation.

The truth is many artists were not focused on expressing their personal emotions or providing definitive answers. Instead, their true intent was often to share—to communicate their unique perspectives and intentions with the world. By exploring the intentions behind various artists and the cultural movements that produced such beautiful works, we can uncover deeper meanings and connections.

The question of intent remains central and profoundly intriguing, as it serves as the foundation upon which all forms of expression are built. This concept extends beyond art, permeating every single aspect of life. In everything we do, we can find the beauty of intent, as it shapes our actions, guides our decisions, and influences our interactions with the world around us.

Vision

———◦❈❈◦———

My goal when writing this book was to introduce the concept of intent not only as a way of viewing life but also as a critical component in business.

How do you convey intent in your business? What are your intentions toward your business—its management, its teams, its leaders, its people, its community, and the world at large? Consider whether your actions are aligned with a vision as expansive and profound as the universe itself.

Reflecting deeply on this can transform your business approach, leading to a vision statement that not only guides but also inspires and elevates every aspect of your organization. Crafting a vision statement can be as simple or as complex as you choose. The key is to understand that while the approach may vary, the ultimate goal remains the same: defining a clear and compelling direction for your business.

Imagine your business as a separate entity from yourself. This separation allows you to see its needs, ambitions, and potential more objectively.

For instance, if you're someone who leans towards stoicism, numbers, and statistics, think of your business as a game—a complex RPG where you're the strategist, guiding your character to achieve its ultimate goal. Remember, the character isn't you; it's just a role you're directing. Your job is to listen to your business's inner voice, just as we listen to our own consciousness.

On the other hand, if you're an entrepreneur driven by feelings and emotions, envision your business as a growing child. This distinction allows you to see the business as its own entity, with its own dreams and aspirations. It gives you the freedom to set it on its unique path.

Why is this helpful? Because it separates your personal identity from your business, granting you the objectivity to steer it effectively. Of course, you're the architect behind it all—the responsibility is yours. But by seeing your business as an independent being, it becomes easier to understand what a true vision statement should encompass. This perspective also frees you from many other constraints and biases, enabling you to approach challenges with a clearer, more focused mindset.

A vision statement serves as a beacon, illuminating the path ahead and ensuring that every decision, every action, aligns with your ultimate goal. It articulates where you see your business in the future and provides a framework for making strategic choices.

Ask yourself: if your business were a child, who would you want it to grow up to be? What changes would it make in the world? If you could set everything up perfectly for future generations, starting with this one business, what would its scope and aspirations be? What is the ultimate end goal?

By defining these elements, you transform abstract ideas into a concrete vision. Whether you see your business as a game to be won or a child to be nurtured, the destination is the same —a successful, purposeful entity that stands the test of time.

Registering your business and finding the right structure is straightforward—think of it as logging into a game or customizing your game avatar. It's the first step, and though it's important, it's not the most challenging part of your journey. The real adventure begins with defining your vision and intent.

This vision statement will be the guiding star for your business, ensuring that every decision, every strategy, and every action propels you towards your ultimate goal.

A vision statement must be concise yet powerful, embodying clarity and decisiveness. Each word should carry intent, reflecting the core aspirations of your business. Aim for goals that are bold, visionary, and seemingly unattainable, goals that challenge the status quo and push the boundaries of possibility. These audacious objectives are not just encouraged but essential for fostering innovation and long-term success. By crafting such a vision statement, you establish a guiding star for your business, ensuring that every decision, strategy, and action aligns with your ultimate goals.

Core Values

While a vision statement illuminates the path forward, it is your core values that form the bedrock upon which your business stands. These values are the fundamental beliefs and guiding principles that influence every decision, action, and interaction within your organization. Imagine your business as a thriving garden, with your core values as the rich, fertile soil that nourishes and sustains every plant. Just as the roots of a tree provide stability and essential nutrients, core values ground your business, shaping its culture and ensuring its growth and resilience. By cultivating a strong foundation of core values, you create an environment where your business can flourish, blossom, and reach its fullest potential.

Your business should be an adventure, much like an immersive MMORPG (Massively Multiplayer Online Role-Playing Game). Your vision is the ultimate destination—a distant, dazzling city on the horizon that you and your team are striving to reach. Core values, however, are the essential tools and maps in your inventory, guiding your journey and ensuring that every step you take is aligned with your ultimate purpose.

Think of core values as the compass that always points true north, and the detailed map that shows every hidden path and obstacle. In the world of video games, these tools are indispensable. They help you navigate complex terrains, avoid pitfalls, and make strategic decisions that keep you on course. Similarly, in your business, core values provide the direction and clarity needed to overcome challenges and stay true to your mission.

In Video Games, players must rely on their skills, tools, and alliances to progress through levels and achieve their goals. Your business operates in much the same way. Core values are the skills and principles that empower your team, build trust with your customers, and create a cohesive and resilient organization. They are the unwavering truths that keep everyone aligned and motivated, even when the journey becomes challenging.

While there are countless core values that can be applied in the business world, there are three main ones that I want to highlight: courage, integrity, and stewardship. Every company should embody these values because they form the foundation for achieving excellence and creating a positive impact.

Your business should never shy away from challenges. Courage empowers your organization to take bold steps, innovate, and grow, even in the face of adversity. It's about making tough decisions and standing firm in your convictions. Just as a hero in a story faces obstacles head-on, your business should approach challenges with bravery and confidence.

This is the backbone of trust and reliability. Integrity ensures that your business operates transparently and ethically. When your company commits to honesty and doing the right thing, it builds a reputation that customers and partners can depend on. Think of integrity as the moral compass that keeps your business on the right path, no matter what.

Stewardship is about responsible management and care for the resources entrusted to your business. It's about making decisions that benefit not just the company, but also your employees, customers, and the broader community. Stewardship ensures that your business contributes positively to society and sustains its success over the long term.

Imagine these values as the guiding principles that inform every decision you make. With courage, integrity, and stewardship at the core, your business can navigate any terrain, much like a skilled adventurer in a video game equipped with the best tools and strategies.

Even if life throws many challenges your way, and we all know how unpredictable life can be, these core values will serve as the pillars that keep your business steady and focused. When your business embodies courage, it will never back down from opportunities. When it upholds integrity, it will always operate with honesty and fairness. And when it practices stewardship, it will ensure that its actions benefit everyone involved.

By instilling these values into your company culture, you create an environment where other positive values can flourish. Courage, integrity, and stewardship set the stage for a thriving, principled business that not only achieves its goals but also makes a meaningful impact.

Brand Identity

Let's discuss the creation of a compelling brand identity. This is the culmination of everything we've covered so far, integrating intent, vision, and core values into a cohesive and powerful brand image. If we think of your brand as a monster or child, how do you want the world to perceive it? What will it wear, how will it speak, and what emotions will it evoke? Your brand identity is the persona your business presents to the world, encompassing visual appearance, communication style, and the values it stands for.

Visualize your brand as a character in a video game. Just as you carefully choose attributes, outfits, and abilities for your game character, you must craft every detail of your brand's identity. How does your character look? What kind of clothes does it wear? What facial expressions does it show, and how does it communicate? These choices define how your character is perceived by other players in the game, much like how your brand is perceived by the world.

Imagine setting up your brand in a character creation screen. You pick its appearance, voice, and even its backstory. These elements combine to create a unique persona. What do people feel when they encounter your brand? What memories or associations does it evoke? These elements are crucial in forming a lasting connection with your audience.

Your brand identity should reflect the unique personality of your business. It's not just about aesthetics; it's about conveying a message and building a relationship with your audience. Consistency is crucial—ensure that your brand's visual elements, tone of voice, and values are harmonized across all platforms and interactions. This coherence strengthens your brand's image and fosters loyalty and trust among your audience.

The importance of understanding your intent and core values cannot be overstated. These foundational elements guide every aspect of your brand identity. Intent drives purpose, giving your brand a clear direction and mission. Core values ensure consistency and integrity in your actions and communications. Together, they create a brand that is not only recognizable but also trusted and respected.

Mission statements play a vital role in keeping your brand on track to achieve its goals. These statements are not static; they can evolve and improve over time, reflecting the growth and learning of your business. However, the essence of your mission should remain constant, grounded in the good intentions that guide your actions. Never quit on your mission because it evolves with you, ensuring that your goals are always aligned with your core values and vision.

Creating a compelling brand identity involves careful consideration and strategic thinking. It's about more than just designing a logo or choosing colors; it's about crafting a persona that resonates with people and stands out in a crowded marketplace. Your brand identity is a reflection of who you are, what you stand for, and where you're headed. By integrating intent, core values, and a clear vision, you can create a brand that not only captures attention but also inspires and connects with your audience on a deeper level.

Your brand identity is the public face of your business, shaped by your intent, vision, and core values. It's how your business is perceived by the world and how it communicates its essence. By meticulously crafting your brand identity and ensuring it aligns with your business's foundational principles, you can create a powerful, cohesive, and compelling brand that leaves a lasting impression and drives your business forward.

0 to 11

―――――❧◆❧―――――

With a solid foundation of core values in place, it's equally important to master the art of decision-making. To help you navigate this crucial aspect of business, I've developed a concept that simplifies the decision-making process into four distinct states. This approach is both straightforward and powerful, providing a clear framework for tackling any choice that comes your way.

0-0; This is the state where you take no action, and nothing happens as a result. It's like being AFK (away from keyboard) in a game—you're not engaging, and therefore, nothing changes. Many people live their lives in this state, passively observing without making any moves. It's easy to fall into this trap because our world is designed to make things easier for us. Every business, every new idea aims to simplify our lives. However, many of us confuse "easier" with "staying put."

The reason the 0-0 state exists is to remind us of this misconception. It's a state of mere existence—beautiful in its simplicity, yes, but ultimately unproductive. Remember when you were a kid, and your biggest worry was deciding what to eat next? That carefree state is often romanticized, and many people long for that simplicity. They fall in love with the idea of staying still, believing it to be a solution to life's complexities.

But here's the trick: while moments of rest and simplicity

have their place, progress and fulfillment come from actively engaging with opportunities and challenges. Imagine your business as a grand adventure in an MMORPG . Just like in a game, standing still won't earn you experience points or help you level up. To advance, you need to engage with the game world, complete quests, and interact with other characters.

The 0-0 state can feel comfortable and safe, much like the nostalgic memories of childhood. However, to truly thrive, you need to move beyond this passive state. Recognize that "easier" should mean facilitating action, not avoiding it. Embrace the journey with courage, integrity, and stewardship. By doing so, you ensure that your business not only survives but flourishes, evolving with every step you take.

In the 0-1 state, an opportunity arises, but you're not there to seize it. This can lead to regret as you realize what you missed out on. It's akin to a missed quest in a game—available but unclaimed because you weren't paying attention. This state is more complex than it appears, and its impact on our psyche can be profound.

Consider this scenario: An opportunity presents itself, but you do nothing. You're not actively pursuing it, so only two outcomes are possible: either you miss the opportunity, or it somehow falls into your lap without effort on your part. We all know those "happy-go-lucky" individuals who seem to land on their feet no matter what. This is why people are drawn to gambling; they like to believe in luck and miracles. And while believing in miracles can be beautiful, relying solely on luck is not a strategy.

But what if the opportunity is missed? This is where regret comes in, one of the most significant psychological burdens we carry. Understanding the 0-1 state helps us see that missed opportunities are not necessarily anyone's fault. You weren't there to make it happen, so there's no one to blame. Yet, the feeling of regret can be powerful and debilitating.

Think of those who spend years studying, doing all the right things, yet still miss out on opportunities. They experience a sense of futility, questioning why their hard work didn't pay off. This brings us to the 1-0 state, where you're putting in the effort and showing up, but the results aren't there. It's frustrating and disheartening, like grinding in a game without progressing. This often happens due to a lack of clear goals or misaligned efforts.

What about the hardworking individuals who pour their energy into their jobs, believing that perseverance alone will bring success? They keep pushing, but nothing seems to change. This state is marked by a relentless pursuit without clear direction. It's the hope that if they just keep working hard, a breakthrough will come.

However, this relentless effort can lead to burnout and disillusionment. Look at our society today: the rising costs of living, education, and basic necessities have created a situation where even those who work tirelessly struggle to get ahead. Many young people are burdened with student loans and degrees that may not guarantee employment. This is the harsh reality of the One-zero.

People in this state feel drained, constantly questioning the value of their efforts. They see others succeeding with seemingly less effort and wonder what they're doing wrong. The frustration of working hard without tangible results can be overwhelming.

The 0-1 and 1-0 states highlight the challenges of missed opportunities and unyielding efforts. Both states can lead to feelings of regret, frustration, and disillusionment. It's important to recognize these states and understand that they are part of the journey.

Remember the 0-0 state, where no action is taken, and nothing changes. The world keeps moving, opportunities continue to exist, but they remain unaffected by your inaction. The key is to avoid getting stuck in the 0-1 and 1-0 states by aligning your efforts with clear goals and being present to seize opportunities.

Now, let's delve into the 1-1 (One-One) state—the ideal state that I want everyone to understand and embrace. This state is about more than just a "do it" mentality; it's about being fully present and open to possibilities. It's about positivity, engagement, and taking charge of your destiny.

The beauty of the 1-1 lies in its dual nature. Firstly, it's you Being there, actively making decisions and crafting your future. You are the sculptor of your destiny, the cause of whatever comes next. This act of creation is powerful and beautiful in and of itself. But there's another aspect: the opportunities that arise. Every decision, every new aspect of life, every unexpected event represents potential. The magic of the 1-1 state is in recognizing and seizing these moments.

Consider the concept of the multiverse and Schrödinger's cat—a thought experiment where a cat in a box can be both alive and dead until observed. In the context of decision-making, the cat and the box represent the second "one" in the 1-1 state. The box contains endless possibilities, but it's your action that determines the outcome.

In the 0-0 state, there is no cat, no box, and no decision. In the 0-1 state, there's a box with a potential cat, but you're not there to open it. It could contain anything—a kitten, a coupon for a million cats, or nothing at all. The opportunity is present, but it's wasted without your engagement.

In the 1-0 state, people wander aimlessly, hoping to find a box someday. They might study boxes, watch videos about cats, or wish for a box to appear, but without a clear target, their efforts yield no results. It's a state of perpetual preparation without action.

The 1-1, however, is when you are there to open the box. You take the initiative. Whether you find a cat, an empty box, or something else entirely, you learn and grow from the experience. Maybe you discover you need to approach the next box differently. Perhaps you become so adept at opening boxes that the contents no longer surprise you but excite you with their potential. The true reward is in the act of opening the box and engaging with what you find.

Embrace the 1-1 with courage and presence. It's where preparation meets opportunity, and where true growth and success occur. By being present and taking action, you turn possibilities into realities, transforming your business and life into a fulfilling adventure.

By embracing the 1-1 state, you fundamentally transform your approach to decision-making and, consequently, the essence of the three core values—courage, integrity, and stewardship.

Courage in the 1-1 state is about more than just facing challenges head-on. It's about being present and proactive in every moment, seizing opportunities as they arise, and not waiting for the perfect moment. It's the courage to take risks, knowing that each decision is a step towards growth and discovery. It's about actively crafting your future, understanding that you are the sculptor of your destiny.

Integrity in the 1-1 state transcends the traditional notion of honesty and ethical behavior. It becomes the guiding force that ensures every decision aligns with your core values and vision. Being present and engaged means that your actions are consistently reflective of your principles, maintaining trust and reliability in every interaction. Integrity is about being true to your mission, even when faced with unexpected opportunities or challenges.

Stewardship in the 1-1 state is about embracing the responsibility to make decisions that benefit not just your business, but also your employees, customers, and the broader community. It's about managing resources wisely and ensuring that every action you take contributes positively to society. In the 1-1 state, stewardship means recognizing the potential in every situation and nurturing it to create value for all stakeholders.

By doing this, you embrace a proactive, engaged, and optimistic approach to business and life. It transforms how you view challenges and opportunities, emphasizing the importance of being present and making intentional, impactful decisions. By living in the 1-1 state, you align your actions with your core values, driving your business towards success and fulfillment.

Ultimately, the 1-1 state brings a new depth to courage, integrity, and stewardship, making these core values more dynamic and integral to your business's journey. It ensures that every step you take is purposeful and aligned with your vision, creating a thriving, principled organization that not only achieves its goals but also makes a meaningful impact on the world.

Systems

———◦❖———

Implementing robust systems is crucial for the success of any business. While many people associate systems with making processes faster, better, or more efficient, the true purpose of a system is much simpler: it's about creating a consistent, understandable framework that anyone can follow. A system is essentially a documented method for performing specific tasks within your business. Whether it's as complex as an IT security protocol or as simple as using different colored pens for different tasks, if it's written down and explained, it's a system.

Let's consider a basic example: if you designate a red pen for signing your name and a black pen for signing official documents, and you document this rule, it becomes a system. This system works because it's clear and understandable. Anyone new to the business can quickly learn and follow the rules, ensuring consistency. The simplicity of the system doesn't diminish its importance; it's effective because it provides clear instructions and removes ambiguity.

The key to successful systems is documentation. Putting your processes on paper makes them real and actionable. It provides a reference point for anyone in your business to understand how things should be done. This is especially important for ensuring continuity and clarity, whether for current employees or future generations.

Operational systems ensure your business runs smoothly. This includes IT systems for securing your business's data, customer relationship management (CRM) systems for managing interactions with customers, and logistical support systems for managing inventory and supply chains. Each of these systems plays a vital role in maintaining the efficiency and security of your operations.

These systems are essential for maintaining transparency and accountability. Despite the importance, many businesses overlook the need to document financial processes, leading to inconsistencies and errors.

To implement effective systems in your business, start by identifying the key processes that need to be standardized. Document each step clearly, explaining the purpose and method. Ensure that these documents are easily accessible to everyone who needs them. This transparency fosters a culture of accountability and efficiency.

Now, let's take this concept to an extreme. Imagine your business as a video game. In a game, everything comes down to zeros and ones—binary code that dictates every action and outcome. As a business owner, you are not just managing operations; you are essentially a coder, creating and refining the systems that drive your business forward. Every rule, every procedure, and every protocol is a line of code that ensures your business functions smoothly and effectively.

If you choose to view your business from different perspectives, you become akin to a doctor. Just as a doctor understands the intricacies of how every organ and cell functions within the body, you must grasp how every aspect of your business operates. This comprehensive understanding allows you to become an expert in your business's systems, capable of diagnosing issues and optimizing performance.

Seeing your business as a game or a living organism highlights the importance of systems. In a game, every action is pre-defined by the code, ensuring consistency and predictability. In a living organism, systems ensure that every part functions harmoniously to maintain health and vitality. By applying these principles to your business, you can create an environment where everything runs like clockwork, guided by clear, well-documented systems.

In summary, systems are essential for any business. They provide a clear, consistent framework for performing tasks, ensuring that everyone understands how things should be done. Whether it's a simple rule about pen colors or a complex IT security protocol, documenting your systems is key to their effectiveness. By implementing and maintaining robust systems, you can ensure that your business operates smoothly and efficiently, paving the way for sustainable growth and success. Embrace the mindset of a coder or a doctor and see your business transform through the power of well-crafted systems.

Money

Implementing official financial systems is crucial for the success and stability of any business. Establishing robust financial protocols and accounting systems to manage cash flows, budgets, and financial reporting accurately is essential, but it goes beyond just the mechanics. It's about shaping the money culture of your company, understanding your relationship with money, and defining how it will be used to drive your business forward.

Financial systems provide the foundation for all business operations. They ensure that every transaction is recorded, every dollar is accounted for, and financial health can be monitored and managed effectively. Without these systems, a business can quickly fall into disarray, making it difficult to track performance, manage expenses, or make informed decisions. At the core of any financial system are the processes for managing cash flows, budgets, and financial reporting. These systems help you understand where your money is coming from, where it's going, and how it's being spent. Accurate financial reporting provides insights into profitability, liquidity, and overall financial health, enabling you to make strategic decisions that drive growth and sustainability.

But implementing financial systems is about more than just numbers. It's about creating a money culture within your organization. This culture reflects your attitudes and beliefs about money and dictates how financial resources are managed and utilized. Consider your company's money culture: Are you scared of money, or do you embrace it? Do you see money as a tool for good, or is it merely a means to an end? Is your focus on enriching the owners, or do you prioritize the well-being of your employees and community?

prioritize the well-being of your employees and community?

Defining your money culture involves asking critical questions: What does money mean to your business? How do you plan to use it to achieve your goals? Are your financial practices aligned with your core values and vision? Understanding the answers to these questions helps you establish a clear financial philosophy that guides your decision-making process.

Once you have a clear understanding of your money culture, you can begin to implement the necessary financial systems. This involves setting up processes for managing capital budgets, financial reporting, and cash flow monitoring. The key is to ensure that these systems are documented and accessible, creating transparency and accountability within your organization.

In today's digital age, businesses have several options for managing their finances. You can employ a dedicated team of accountants or leverage AI and other technological solutions to streamline financial management. Regardless of the method, the important thing is to have everything documented. This documentation transforms your financial practices from abstract concepts into concrete policies, ensuring consistency and reliability in how money is handled.

By putting your financial protocols and accounting systems on paper, you create a tangible framework that governs your financial operations. This is not just for internal use but also for stakeholders who need to understand your financial health and strategies. Having clear, accessible financial documentation ensures that everyone involved in your business, from employees to investors, is on the same page.

Establishing robust financial systems is essential for managing your business effectively. It's about more than just tracking money—it's about understanding and defining your relationship with money and using it to create a thriving, principled business. By embracing a clear money culture, implementing well-documented financial systems, and leveraging technology, you can ensure that your business not only survives but flourishes, driving growth and making a positive impact.

Paper

———◦∞❈∞◦———

Entrepreneurship is a journey filled with excitement, challenges, and numerous decisions that shape the future of your business. One of the critical aspects often overlooked by new entrepreneurs is the importance of legal protection and risk management. While it's tempting to trust everyone at face value, experience teaches us that such an approach can be risky. It's a sad reality that living with distrust is exhausting, yet in business, there's simply no time for trial and error. Trust everyone completely until they start showing you who they are, but ensure you have every critical detail documented. Before diving into building a team, it's essential to establish a strong legal foundation to safeguard your business. Contracts, agreements, and clear protocols will provide the necessary security and clarity, allowing you to operate confidently and focus on growing your venture.

As a business owner, your first priority should be to protect your business legally. Establishing a robust legal framework is crucial for mitigating risks and ensuring long-term success. This starts with choosing the appropriate legal structure for your business, whether it's a sole proprietorship, partnership, LLC, or corporation. This decision impacts your liability, taxes, and regulatory obligations. Ensuring compliance with all local, state, and federal regulations is vital to avoid legal issues down the road.

Drafting clear and comprehensive contracts for your business relationships is another critical step. Employee agreements, vendor contracts, and partnership agreements should outline the terms and conditions of each party's responsibilities, reducing the risk of misunderstandings and disputes. Additionally, safeguarding your business's intellectual property (IP) by securing trademarks, copyrights, and patents is essential. Protecting your IP ensures that your brand, products, and innovations remain exclusively yours.

Implementing risk management strategies to identify, assess, and mitigate potential risks is also necessary. This includes purchasing adequate insurance coverage for property, liability, and employee protection, as well as developing contingency plans for unforeseen events. Retaining a knowledgeable attorney to guide you through legal matters and provide ongoing advice is invaluable. Having a legal expert on your team can help you navigate complex legal landscapes and make informed decisions.

With a solid legal and risk management foundation in place, you can confidently focus on the next critical aspect of your business: building a team. One of the biggest challenge business owners face is assembling a team. The uncertainty of hiring new employees and integrating them into your company can be daunting. However, building a strong team is essential for growth and success.

Understand that hiring is an integral part of business growth. While it's challenging to predict how new hires will fit into your company, approach the process with an open mind and a strategic plan. Look beyond resumes; while they provide valuable information, they don't tell the whole story. Focus on finding candidates whose values align with your company's culture and who demonstrate potential for growth and adaptability.

Create a work environment where employees feel valued and respected. Encourage collaboration, open communication, and continuous learning. A positive culture attracts and retains top talent. Don't let fear hold you back from making necessary changes. If a team member isn't working out, address the issue promptly and make the needed adjustments. Similarly, be open to changing your approach if it benefits the team.

Surround yourself with people you respect and believe in. Trust is built over time, but starting with a foundation of respect can lead to strong, productive relationships. Ensure that all employment practices comply with labor laws and regulations. This includes fair hiring practices, employee rights, and workplace safety. Addressing legal aspects early on prevents potential issues and fosters a fair work environment. Utilize tools and strategies to facilitate clear and effective communication within your team. Transparency and honesty are crucial for building trust and ensuring everyone is on the same page.

By integrating these strategies, you can build a team that is not only skilled but also aligned with your business's core values and vision. Remember, a successful team is dynamic and adaptable, ready to face challenges and seize opportunities. Bringing together legal protection and team building creates a solid foundation for your business. Legal and risk management ensure that your business is safeguarded from potential threats, allowing you to focus on growth and innovation. Meanwhile, a strong team drives your business forward, executing your vision and contributing to a positive company culture.

Once you have a solid foundation and a strong team in place, the next step is monitoring and making necessary adjustments to your strategies and operations. Establishing mechanisms for tracking performance and creating feedback loops is essential for continuous improvement. Regular reviews, whether weekly, monthly, or quarterly, help assess both qualitative and quantitative data, providing a comprehensive view of your business's performance. Encouraging open communication within your team to gather insights and suggestions fosters a culture of continuous learning and adaptation.

Adjustments are necessary because no plan remains perfect forever. Market conditions change, customer preferences evolve, and new opportunities emerge. Being able to pivot and adapt ensures that your business stays relevant and competitive. Just as a living organism evolves, your business must also be capable of evolving based on the feedback and data collected.

A growth plan outlines your business's path for future expansion, including new markets, products, and services you need to explore. Having a growth plan is more than just setting goals; it's about creating a roadmap for achieving those goals and being prepared to evolve along the way. The growth plan should begin with a vision statement that is ambitious and almost unreachable. This sets a high bar and motivates your team to strive for excellence. The mission statements are the steps that guide you toward this vision. These should be specific, measurable, achievable, relevant, and time-bound (SMART). Each mission statement should address a particular aspect of your business growth, whether it's entering a new market, launching a new product, or improving operational efficiency. Once a mission is accomplished, a new one should be created to continue driving progress. If a mission proves unattainable, it should be revised and adjusted to better align with your evolving business landscape.

Documenting your growth plan on paper is crucial. Just like having systems in place, a written growth plan ensures that everyone involved understands the goals and strategies. It provides a clear guide for employees, stakeholders, and even customers, aligning their efforts towards common objectives. Regardless of your ultimate goal—whether you plan to grow the company to pass it down through generations or prepare it for an exit strategy like a sale—the growth plan provides the structure needed to reach those objectives. The clarity provided by a documented plan ensures that your team and stakeholders can effectively contribute to achieving your vision.

Duality

D uality is a fundamental concept that underpins the very fabric of existence. It manifests itself in every aspect of life, from the natural world to human consciousness, and plays a critical role in the realm of business. Understanding duality means appreciating the interplay of opposing forces that drive growth, innovation, and balance.

At its core, duality acknowledges that two contrasting elements must coexist to create something new. This principle is evident in science, where matter and antimatter, positive and negative charges, and other opposing forces interact to form the universe. In biology, life itself arises from the combination of diverse elements, and in physics, the dance of opposites creates the dynamic equilibrium that sustains the cosmos.

Religions and philosophies across cultures also recognize the significance of duality. From the yin and yang in Taoism, representing harmony through the balance of opposites, to the biblical notion of light and darkness, duality is seen as essential to the existence and understanding of life. Even in language, we find duality in antonyms and synonyms, shaping the way we communicate and comprehend the world around us.

For the entrepreneur, embracing duality means recognizing and balancing these opposing forces within their business. It's about understanding that strength and vulnerability, tradition and innovation, consistency and adaptability, are not mutually exclusive but rather complementary. This balance is crucial for creating a resilient and dynamic organization.

Consider the role of duality in decision-making. Every choice involves weighing the pros and cons, risks and rewards. By acknowledging duality, you can make more nuanced and effective decisions, blending caution with boldness to navigate the complexities of the business landscape.

In leadership, duality manifests as the balance between authority and empathy. A successful leader must be decisive and strong, yet also compassionate and understanding. This dual approach fosters a healthy work environment and drives team performance.

In innovation, duality is about honoring the past while embracing the future. It's about maintaining the core values that define your brand while being open to new ideas and technologies that propel your business forward. This balance ensures that your company remains relevant and competitive in a rapidly changing market.

As you reflect on these ideas, ask yourself: How do the dualities in my business interact? Are there areas where I am favoring one side over the other? How can I create a more harmonious balance that drives growth and innovation?

The answers may not be straightforward, and that's the beauty of duality—it invites us to explore, question, and adapt. By embracing this principle, you open your business to new possibilities and create a foundation for sustained success.

Skills

———◦✦❈✦◦———

N ow that we've introduced the concept of duality, let's delve into a new framework for understanding skills, which I call the "Anatomy of a Skill." This methodology breaks down any skill into three fundamental components: innate traits, earned elements, and environmental influences. Together, these aspects provide a deeper, more comprehensive understanding of how skills are developed and mastered.

Consider the act of breathing as an illustrative example. Breathing is a fundamental skill essential for life and universally present among all living beings. At its core, breathing exemplifies the innate traits we are born with. From the moment we enter the world, the ability to breathe is hardwired into our biology. This core gift is not something we learn; it is an intrinsic part of our existence, a fundamental trait that sustains life.

Beyond innate traits, we encounter environmental influences that shape how we breathe. These influences encompass everything in our surroundings that impacts our understanding and practice of breathing. For instance, observing how animals breathe, witnessing the rhythmic rise and fall of a pet's chest, or experiencing different breathing patterns in various cultural or familial contexts all contribute to our environmental understanding of breathing. These shaped traits form a repository of experiences and observations that subtly influence our own breathing habits.

The third component, earned elements, represents the aspects of the skill we intentionally develop through practice and learning. This is where conscious effort and intent come into play. While everyone is born with the ability to breathe, mastering the skill of breathing requires deliberate practice and knowledge. Consider techniques such as deep breathing exercises used to calm the mind or specific breathing patterns employed in yoga and meditation. These techniques are not innate; they are learned and honed through experience and practice. Earned elements are where the mind actively engages, connects dots, and refines a skill through intentional action.

To truly master a skill, it is not enough to rely solely on innate traits or environmental influences. Mastery requires the integration and understanding of all three components. Innate traits provide the foundation, environmental influences offer context and variability, and earned elements represent the culmination of focused practice and learning. This triad ensures a well-rounded and profound understanding of any skill.

Applying this methodology to breathing reveals the depth and complexity of what might initially seem like a simple act. Breathing is something we all do instinctively, yet the way we breathe can significantly impact our health, well-being, and mental state. There are individuals who have dedicated their lives to mastering the art of breathing, such as monks and breathing experts, who believe that proper breathing techniques can heal and transform the body and mind. These masters of breathing exemplify the pinnacle of integrating innate traits, environmental influences, and earned elements to achieve extraordinary control and understanding of the skill.

This framework can be applied to any skill, offering a structured way to analyze and develop expertise. Whether it's learning a musical instrument, mastering a sport, or excelling in a professional domain, understanding the anatomy of a skill allows for a holistic approach to skill development. It encourages us to recognize the innate traits we possess, appreciate the environmental factors that have shaped us, and commit to the ongoing process of learning and practice.

To truly master a skill, it's essential to identify and understand the level at which each of these aspects—innate traits, earned elements, and environmental influences—impacts your ability. Recognizing where you stand with each component allows for a comprehensive approach to skill development. For example, if you know you have an innate ability to grasp complex concepts quickly, you can focus more on enhancing your study techniques and creating a conducive environment to maximize your potential.

Identifying the degree to which each aspect influences your skill development is crucial. By doing so, you can pinpoint areas that need more attention and effort. If your earned elements, such as specific study techniques, are lacking, you can invest time in learning and practicing new methods. Similarly, if your environment is not supportive, you can make changes to create a more conducive study space.

Understanding the anatomy of a skill and evaluating the influence of each component allows you to take a targeted approach to mastery. It's not just about practicing a skill repeatedly; it's about understanding the underlying factors that contribute to your proficiency. This holistic view ensures that you address all aspects of skill development, leading to more effective and sustained mastery.

The anatomy of a skill provides a comprehensive methodology for understanding and mastering any ability. By examining the interplay between innate traits, environmental influences, and earned elements over time, we gain a deeper appreciation of the complexities involved in skill development. This approach not only enhances our understanding but also empowers us to achieve mastery through intentional and informed practice. As you explore and apply this framework, you will uncover new depths to your abilities and unlock the potential for continuous growth and excellence.

Creative

Whenpeople think of creativity, they often envision artists, musicians, and writers—those who conjure ideas from thin air and transform them into something tangible and inspiring. On the other hand, business is frequently associated with numbers, strategies, and precise calculations. The common misconception is that creativity and business are mutually exclusive realms, with little overlap between the two. However, this couldn't be further from the truth. Creativity is not only compatible with business, but it is also an essential component for entrepreneurial success.

For entrepreneurs or those contemplating starting a business, understanding the role of creativity is vital. Creativity fuels innovation and generates novel solutions, driving transformative processes within a business. It is the spark that ignites new ideas, products, and services. But creativity alone is not enough. To truly succeed, these creative impulses must be grounded in analytical skills, providing a structural framework that translates imaginative concepts into actionable, measurable outcomes.

Creative skills are characterized by their ability to think outside the box, challenge the status quo, and envision possibilities beyond the conventional. This imaginative thinking is crucial for developing unique products, services, and strategies that set a business apart from its competitors. Creativity fosters a culture of innovation, where new ideas are encouraged, explored, and implemented. It drives the dynamic processes that lead to breakthroughs and advancements, enabling businesses to adapt and thrive in an ever-changing market.

Conversely, analytical skills are the foundation that supports and structures these creative impulses. Precision, data analysis, and strategic planning are essential for transforming creative ideas into viable business solutions. Analytical skills provide the tools to evaluate the feasibility of creative concepts, measure their potential impact, and develop actionable plans for implementation. They ensure that innovative ideas are not just imaginative but also practical and effective.

The fusion of creativity and precision is a dual force that transforms vision into reality. When entrepreneurs harness both creative and analytical skills, they create a powerful synergy that drives sustained growth and advancement. This combination allows for the development of innovative solutions that are both groundbreaking and executable.

Consider the development of a new product. Creativity sparks the initial idea, envisioning a unique solution to a problem or a novel feature that sets the product apart. Analytical skills then come into play, evaluating market demand, conducting feasibility studies, and developing a business plan to bring the product to market. This dual approach ensures that the product is not only innovative but also market-ready and poised for success.

Incorporating creativity into business practices also fosters a more engaging and dynamic workplace culture. Employees are encouraged to think creatively, contribute new ideas, and participate in the innovation process. This inclusive approach not only enhances job satisfaction and morale but also drives collective progress and success.

On the flip side, individuals who are naturally creative must also develop their analytical skills to succeed in business. Understanding market dynamics, financial planning, and strategic decision-making are crucial for turning creative ideas into profitable ventures. By balancing creativity with precision, creative individuals can navigate the complexities of the business world and achieve their entrepreneurial goals.

Creativity and business are not opposing forces but complementary components that, when combined, create a powerful synergy. Creativity drives innovation, while analytical skills provide the structure and precision needed to turn imaginative ideas into actionable, measurable outcomes. For entrepreneurs and aspiring business owners, embracing both creativity and precision is essential for transforming vision into reality, fostering sustained growth, and driving enduring success. By harnessing the dual forces of creativity and precision, you can unlock the full potential of your business and pave the way for transformative advancements.

Creativity serves as the lifeblood of innovation. However, creativity alone is not enough. To truly differentiate yourself in a competitive market, individuality is crucial. Individuality is not just about thinking differently; it's about acting differently. It's what sets your business apart from the competition and infuses it with a unique identity. This distinctiveness not only attracts clients but also instills pride in employees, creating a loyal and motivated workforce.

Individual

Individuality in business is akin to forging your own path in a complex, ever-changing landscape. While many businesses adhere to established norms and best practices, true distinction arises from daring to be different, exploring new ideas, and embracing unique approaches. This willingness to stand apart from the crowd can be both a strength and a challenge, but it is essential for lasting success and growth.

Individuality is the essence that differentiates your business from others. It is reflected in your brand, your products, and your company culture. When a business embodies individuality, it sends a clear message to clients and employees alike: this is a company that values uniqueness, embraces change, and is unafraid to take risks. This distinctive identity fosters a sense of pride and loyalty among those associated with the business. Employees feel a deeper connection to their work, knowing they are part of something unique and meaningful. Clients appreciate the originality and authenticity, which strengthens their loyalty and trust.

However, individuality comes with its own set of challenges and risks. Being different means stepping away from the safety of the herd, venturing into unknown territories, and facing uncertainties. But this is where true innovation lies. The willingness to take risks and explore new possibilities is what drives progress and sets successful businesses apart from the rest.

For the entrepreneur, individuality is about more than just standing out. It's about staying true to one's values and vision, even when it means going against the grain. It requires courage, resilience, and a willingness to embrace failure as a part of the learning process. By fostering a culture that values individuality, businesses can create an environment where innovation thrives, and employees feel empowered to bring their unique perspectives and ideas to the table.

Imagine a business landscape where every company followed the same blueprint. Innovation would stagnate, and the market would be saturated with indistinguishable products and services. Individuality disrupts this monotony, introducing fresh ideas and new ways of thinking. It challenges the status quo and inspires others to break free from conventional constraints.

Individuality in business also extends to the personal traits of the entrepreneur. It encompasses the unique qualities, passions, and perspectives that you bring to your venture. Your individual approach to problem-solving, leadership, and vision are all integral to your business's success. Embracing these personal attributes and allowing them to shape your business can lead to a more authentic and compelling brand.

Consider, for example, a tech startup founded by someone passionate about environmental sustainability. This entrepreneur's unique perspective might lead the company to develop eco-friendly technologies or adopt sustainable business practices. This individuality not only sets the business apart but also attracts like-minded clients and employees who share the same values.

While individuality is crucial, it's also important to acknowledge that working with proven models is not inherently bad. Many successful businesses have thrived by following established practices and methodologies that have stood the test of time. These models provide a solid foundation and can offer valuable insights and strategies. However, there is always room for improvement and innovation within these frameworks. The key is to blend what is known to work with fresh, innovative ideas that push the boundaries and create new opportunities.

Individuality is a powerful force that can propel a business to new heights. It is the act of thinking and acting differently, of daring to explore new possibilities in a world full of change. By championing individuality, you can create a business that not only stands out in a crowded market but also inspires pride and loyalty in employees and clients alike. Embrace your unique qualities, take the necessary risks, and let your individuality shine. This approach will not only differentiate your business but also pave the way for enduring success and growth. At the same time, don't be afraid to incorporate proven models and strategies. They provide a strong foundation upon which you can build and innovate, ensuring that your business remains both grounded and forward-thinking. By combining the best of both worlds—established practices and unique individuality—you can achieve a balance that leads to lasting success.

Lead

Success is often measured by visible outcomes—growth figures, innovation benchmarks, and team productivity. Yet, beneath this surface of achievements lies the true engine of leadership effectiveness: a profound understanding of motivation. Leadership is less about the authority one wields and more about the insights one harbors into the human spirit. This exploration seeks to unravel the subtle yet powerful dynamics of motivation that can transform potential into performance. It is crafted for those who aspire not just to manage but to truly lead.

As an entrepreneur, understanding and harnessing these motivators is essential for translating leadership into effective business strategies. The most impactful leaders leverage both intrinsic and extrinsic motivators to drive their teams, influencing every aspect of their leadership—from strategy formulation to daily interactions. Here, you will learn how to discern the underlying motivations of your team members and align these with your organizational goals. We will explore practical strategies for fostering an environment where motivation thrives and where every team member feels genuinely engaged and valued.

Achievement is a powerful motivator. The drive to achieve can propel individuals to great heights, but it can also lead to burnout if not managed properly. As a leader, fostering a culture where achievements are celebrated can inspire your team to reach their full potential. However, it's crucial to handle this ethically; the pursuit of achievement can sometimes border on manipulation. Encouraging your team to set and achieve personal and professional goals can lead to a more motivated and productive workforce, but always ensures that this pursuit remains healthy and sustainable.

Affiliation, the human need to belong to a group, is a fundamental motivator because humans are inherently social beings. Creating a sense of belonging within your team can significantly boost morale and productivity. This involves fostering a collaborative environment where team members feel valued and connected. A united team can overcome obstacles more effectively than individuals working in isolation. However, be cautious of fostering an environment where conformity stifles individuality. Encourage collaboration, but also celebrate individual contributions.

Power and influence are classic motivators, often associated with leadership. Understanding power dynamics within your team and organization is vital for effective leadership. Power can inspire and lead, but it must be wielded with intent and integrity. Influence, much like power, should be used strategically to guide your team toward common goals. The intent behind power and influence determines their impact—whether they uplift and empower or control and dominate. Be mindful of the fine line between leadership and tyranny.

Security is a fundamental human need. Everyone wants to feel safe and secure, both in their personal lives and in the workplace. As a leader, creating a secure environment where your team feels safe to express ideas, take risks, and grow is essential. This involves not only physical safety but also job security and a stable, supportive work environment. However, beware of creating a comfort zone that stifles innovation. Balance security with opportunities for growth and challenge.

Curiosity and the desire to learn are powerful motivators. Encouraging a culture of continuous learning and curiosity can lead to innovation and growth. As a leader, fostering an environment where questioning and exploration are encouraged can help your team stay ahead of the curve. Everyone should be curious at all times; the moment we stop asking questions, we stop growing. However, unbridled curiosity can lead to distraction and inefficiency. Guide curiosity with clear goals and objectives.

Autonomy is one of the best motivators. Giving your team the freedom to make decisions and take ownership of their work can lead to higher engagement and productivity. Autonomy fosters a sense of ownership and responsibility, driving individuals to perform at their best. However, too much autonomy without accountability can lead to chaos. Ensure that autonomy is balanced with clear expectations and support.

Recognition and reward are strong motivators that should be carefully understood and utilized. People want to be recognized for their efforts and rewarded for their achievements. This recognition can take many forms, from verbal praise to tangible rewards. Understanding what motivates your team members on an individual level allows you to tailor your recognition and reward systems to be most effective. However, be aware that over-reliance on rewards can lead to a transactional mindset, where team members are motivated only by the next reward. Ensure that recognition is genuine and aligns with the values of your team and organization.

Self-actualization, the realization of one's full potential, is a profound motivator. As a leader, creating an environment where team members can pursue self-actualization benefits both of them individually and the organization collectively. Encouraging personal growth, providing opportunities for professional development, and fostering a culture of continuous improvement are ways to support self-actualization within your team. However, the pursuit of self-actualization can sometimes lead to conflicts with organizational goals. Balance individual aspirations with collective objectives.

Competition can drive individuals to excel and push beyond

their limits. However, the focus should be on healthy competition, where individuals strive to outperform their past selves rather than undermine their peers. As a leader, fostering a culture of personal growth and improvement rather than cutthroat competition can lead to a more supportive and productive work environment. Be cautious of fostering a toxic competitive environment that breeds resentment and burnout.

Fear of failure is a common motivator, but it should be approached with caution. While the fear of failure can drive people to achieve, it can also lead to stress and anxiety. As a leader, it's important to create a culture where failure is seen as a learning opportunity rather than a disaster. Encouraging a growth mindset, where setbacks are viewed as part of the learning process, can help your team overcome the fear of failure and embrace challenges with confidence. However, be wary of inadvertently creating an environment where failure is not tolerated, stifling innovation and risk-taking.

The spirit of adventure and exploration should never die. Encouraging your team to be adventurous, explore new ideas and opportunities, and take calculated risks can lead to innovation and growth. Life is full of possibilities, and fostering a culture where curiosity and exploration are valued can keep your team engaged and motivated. However, ensure that this adventurous spirit is balanced with strategic planning and risk management to avoid reckless decisions.

Status remains an important motivator, even in the age of social media. While status may not be as overtly significant as it once was, it still plays a role in how people perceive themselves and their place in the world. Understanding the role of status in motivation can help you navigate social dynamics within your team and leverage it to drive performance and engagement. However, be cautious of creating a status-driven culture that undermines collaboration and equality.

Altruism and the desire to help others are powerful motivators. Encouraging a culture of altruism within your team can lead to a more collaborative and supportive work environment. When team members are motivated by a desire to help others and contribute to the greater good, it fosters a sense of community and shared purpose. However, be mindful of the potential for burnout among those who prioritize others' needs over their own. Balance altruism with self-care and personal well-being.

Understanding these motivators and how they influence behavior is key to effective leadership. By fostering an environment where these motivators are recognized and leveraged, you can create a thriving, engaged, and productive team. Leadership is about more than just directing others; it's about inspiring them to reach their full potential and aligning their personal goals with the objectives of the organization.

Whether through the pursuit of achievement, the need for affiliation, the drive for power and influence, or the desire for security and autonomy, each motivator plays a critical role in shaping behavior and performance. By recognizing and addressing these motivators, leaders can create an environment where their team thrives. The fusion of intrinsic and extrinsic motivators forms the bedrock of effective leadership, transforming vision into reality and fostering enduring growth and success. Embrace these insights and let them guide you in becoming a leader who not only manages but truly inspires and leads.

Groups

——o——◈——◈——◈——o——

The true measure of a company's success extends beyond financial metrics and productivity figures. It encompasses the well-being of its employees, the strength of its community bonds, and the overall health of the organizational environment. The following transformative strategies can help businesses foster a dynamic workplace characterized by empathy, respect, and mutual growth. By appreciating the importance of these strategies, business owners can cultivate a culture of care that not only drives performance but also enhances employee satisfaction and personal well-being.

Adapting these strategies in contemporary settings is crucial for enhancing performance and employee satisfaction. In a business environment that values both innovation and compassion, the following initiatives can serve as a blueprint for fostering a culture of care and appreciation.

Emotional intelligence is the cornerstone of effective leadership and a harmonious workplace. To amplify emotional intelligence across all levels of the organization, businesses should conduct immersive workshops and regular training sessions aimed at cultivating empathy, active listening, and expressive communication skills. These techniques enhance interpersonal interactions and emotional attunement within teams, leading to improved collaboration and conflict resolution. This approach helps maintain a positive organizational culture in the long run, ensuring that employees feel understood and valued. However, be mindful that high emotional intelligence can also be used manipulatively if not anchored in genuine care and integrity.

Strengthening bonds with the community and building a positive organizational image are essential for long-term success. Implementing sustainable initiatives that involve employees in volunteer efforts, environmental conservation, and community enrichment activities can significantly elevate a company's reputation and employee engagement. Meaningful community interaction fosters a sense of purpose and belonging among employees, reinforcing their connection to the company. By showing genuine care for the community, businesses can build stronger, more resilient relationships both internally and externally. However, ensure that these efforts are authentic and not just performative acts to improve public image.

Solidifying team cohesion and fostering mutual respect among employees are vital for a supportive work environment. Organizing engaging team-building retreats and problem-solving challenges encourages cooperation and innovation. These activities develop stronger team dynamics, enhance mutual respect, and create a supportive and inclusive workplace culture. In the long run, these initiatives contribute to a stable and cohesive team that can weather challenges and seize opportunities with a united front. Beware, though, that team-building efforts should not become mere formalities but genuine efforts to build lasting connections.

Transparency and openness within organizational communication channels are critical for building trust. Maintaining consistent, open lines of communication regarding company policies, updates, and changes promotes an open-door policy with leadership. This framework encourages a culture of openness, proactive feedback, and mutual understanding, which are essential for maintaining a healthy organizational environment. Transparent communication ensures that employees are always informed and involved, fostering a sense of ownership and loyalty. However, transparency must be balanced with discretion to protect sensitive information.

Creating an environment where appreciation is a norm, and employees feel valued, is fundamental to a positive organizational culture. Implementing a robust system of recognition that celebrates both small victories and major accomplishments in varied settings motivates employees and reinforces a positive organizational culture. Recognition and reward are strong motivators that should be carefully understood and utilized. People want to be recognized for their efforts and rewarded for their achievements. Understanding what motivates your team members on an individual level allows you to tailor your recognition and reward systems to be most effective. Nonetheless, be cautious of fostering an environment where recognition feels superficial or insincere.

Addressing and resolving interpersonal conflicts swiftly and effectively is crucial for preserving a harmonious work atmosphere. Offering comprehensive conflict resolution training and establishing a formal process for managing disputes ensures that conflicts are resolved constructively, promoting long-term cooperation and a positive work environment. By tackling issues head-on and with empathy, businesses can maintain a peaceful and productive atmosphere where employees feel heard and respected. However, avoid creating an overly confrontational environment where conflicts are blown out of proportion.

Supporting work-life balance through flexible work arrangements is essential for attracting and retaining top talent. Allowing flexibility in work hours, remote working options, and provisions for mental health days accommodates diverse personal needs and lifestyles, contributing to a more satisfied and productive workforce. A flexible work environment shows employees that the company values their well-being, which can lead to increased loyalty and reduced turnover. Ensure that flexibility does not compromise accountability and productivity.

Encouraging professional growth and knowledge sharing within the organization enhances professional development and builds a supportive learning environment. Pairing seasoned professionals with emerging talent in mentorship relationships facilitates direct knowledge transfer and career development, fostering a culture of continuous improvement and growth. By investing in the growth of its employees, a business can ensure that it remains innovative and competitive in the long run. Beware of creating an environment where growth opportunities are perceived as unfairly distributed.

Promoting a workplace where diversity is celebrated, and inclusivity is ingrained is essential for fostering innovation and maintaining a globally competitive organization. Developing comprehensive training and policies that enhance understanding and respect for diverse backgrounds and perspectives creates an environment where all employees feel valued and included. A diverse and inclusive workplace harnesses a wide range of talents and ideas, driving creativity and performance. However, ensure that diversity efforts are substantive and not just token gestures.

Implementing and tracking diversity and inclusion metrics is essential for measuring the effectiveness of initiatives aimed at fostering an inclusive workplace. These metrics can include the representation of different demographic groups, employee satisfaction surveys, and diversity training participation rates. By regularly evaluating and adjusting their strategies based on these metrics, businesses can ensure they are making meaningful progress towards inclusivity. A diverse and inclusive workplace harnesses a wide range of talents and perspectives, driving creativity, innovation, and overall organizational performance.

Implementing comprehensive employee wellness programs is essential for promoting the overall well-being of your workforce. These programs can include health and wellness initiatives, mental health support, fitness activities, and stress management workshops. By prioritizing employee health, businesses can reduce absenteeism, increase productivity, and create a happier, more engaged workforce. A robust wellness program demonstrates a company's commitment to the holistic health of its employees, fostering a positive and supportive work environment.

Structured career development plans provide employees with clear pathways for growth and advancement within the organization. These plans should outline potential career trajectories, necessary skills and qualifications, and opportunities for professional development. By investing in employees' long-term career growth, businesses can enhance job satisfaction, reduce turnover, and cultivate a highly skilled and motivated workforce. Career development plans also help align individual aspirations with organizational goals, creating a win-win situation for both employees and the company.

Establishing regular feedback mechanisms is crucial for continuous improvement and employee engagement. Implementing formal and informal feedback loops allows employees to voice their opinions, share ideas, and receive constructive feedback. This open exchange fosters a culture of transparency, trust, and mutual respect. Regular feedback helps identify areas for improvement, recognize achievements, and ensure that employees feel valued and heard. By maintaining effective feedback loops, businesses can adapt to changing needs and enhance overall organizational performance.

Providing employees with the necessary technology and tools is fundamental for optimizing productivity and comfort.

Investing in up-to-date software, hardware, and ergonomic equipment ensures that employees have the resources they need to perform their tasks efficiently and comfortably. A well-equipped workplace not only enhances job performance but also shows employees that the company values their work and well-being. Staying current with technological advancements can also drive innovation and keep the organization competitive in a rapidly evolving market.

Engaging in Corporate Social Responsibility (CSR) activities builds a positive image and strengthens community ties. By participating in initiatives such as environmental conservation, charitable contributions, and community service, businesses demonstrate their commitment to social and environmental causes. CSR activities foster a sense of purpose and pride among employees, enhance the company's reputation, and contribute to a positive organizational culture. Businesses that prioritize CSR can attract like-minded clients and employees, creating a more engaged and motivated workforce.

Creating innovation labs or think tanks within the organization provides a dedicated space for brainstorming and developing new ideas. These creative environments encourage employees to explore innovative projects beyond their usual tasks, fostering a culture of experimentation and growth. By supporting these initiatives, businesses can drive continuous improvement, stay ahead of industry trends, and enhance their competitive edge. Innovation labs empower employees to take risks and contribute to the company's long-term success through groundbreaking ideas and solutions.

In conclusion, these transformative strategies reflect how businesses should care for their people and themselves. By amplifying emotional intelligence, strengthening community bonds, solidifying team cohesion, maintaining transparent communication, recognizing achievements, resolving conflicts, supporting work-life balance, fostering professional growth, and promoting inclusivity, businesses can create a dynamic and supportive workplace. This commitment to care not only enhances performance and employee satisfaction but also builds a foundation for sustained success and growth. Embrace these strategies and let them guide your journey toward creating a truly caring and thriving business culture.

By implementing these techniques with love and genuine care, business owners can ensure that their businesses remain vibrant and resilient. These practices will help maintain a positive and productive organizational culture for years to come. Ultimately, these strategies are not just about immediate improvements but about building a sustainable and nurturing environment where both the business and its people can thrive together.

Communication

———◦⊱❈⊰◦———

E ffective communication is a cornerstone of successful business operations. To truly master it, one must understand not only the bright side of honest dialogue and active listening but also the darker aspects of communication. This chapter delves into the nuances of silence, dishonesty, and judgment, offering insights into how these elements can be harnessed to enhance communication skills for business owners and entrepreneurs.

Understanding when to speak and when to listen is a fundamental aspect of communication. Silence, often overlooked, is one of the most powerful tools available. In the rush to fill conversational gaps, we can miss out on the profound impact of silence. When you stay silent and listen, it gives you the time not only to absorb what is being said but also to reflect and think critically about your response. Silence after someone asks you a question signals that you are genuinely considering your answer, demonstrating thoughtfulness and respect. Mastering silence allows you to gauge the conversation better and decide the appropriate moment to contribute, ensuring your words carry weight and relevance.

Dishonesty, or lying, is another critical topic in communication. In the realm of business, as in life, absolute truth is a complex and often elusive concept. Everything is relative, and we can only strive to be as truthful as we perceive ourselves to be. Therefore, our goal should be to avoid dishonesty—towards ourselves, our customers, our colleagues, and our employees. This does not mean we must reveal every detail at all times but rather that we should avoid deceit and manipulation. A subtle form of dishonesty is "crazy talk" or using technical jargon and synonyms to obscure the truth. This can confuse people and lead to misunderstandings. As a business owner, clarity and transparency should be prioritized to build trust and credibility.

Judgment is another critical aspect of communication that requires careful consideration. Everyone has their own opinions and biases, and it is impossible to completely eliminate judgment. However, in a business context, it is crucial to manage and moderate these judgments. Before expressing opinions or critiques, business owners should exercise self-judgment. Reflecting on our own biases and ensuring our comments are constructive and fair can prevent unnecessary conflicts and foster a more positive and collaborative environment. By being mindful of how and when we express our judgments, we can create a more respectful and effective communication culture.

By understanding the darker sides of communication—silence, dishonesty, and judgment—we gain a more comprehensive view of how to communicate effectively. Recognizing the power of silence, striving to avoid dishonesty, and managing judgment can significantly enhance our ability to connect with others and lead with integrity.

In the upcoming sections, we will explore practical tools and methods that not only enhance regular communication but also serve as a comprehensive rubric for generating ideas more quickly and structuring them more effectively. These techniques will improve our business relationships and overall interactions. By mastering these skills, business owners and entrepreneurs can navigate the complexities of communication with greater ease, ensuring that their messages are clear, respectful, and impactful. Integrating these insights and strategies will foster a culture of transparency, trust, and mutual respect within your business.

Effective communication is crucial for the success of any business. It extends beyond the basics of speaking and listening; it involves understanding the deeper structures that can make or break a conversation. In this chapter, we will delve into three powerful techniques for structuring communication: past-present-future, what-so what-what now, and problem-solution-benefits. These techniques will not only enhance everyday interactions but also serve as comprehensive frameworks for generating ideas and structuring them more effectively in business relationships.

To truly master these communication techniques, it is essential to understand three foundational concepts: cause and effect, narrative, and juxtaposition. These elements provide the backbone for presenting ideas clearly and persuasively. Understanding cause and effect is fundamental to any form of communication. It involves identifying the reasons behind events (causes) and their outcomes (effects). In a business context, this means being able to trace the roots of problems, understand their implications, and communicate these insights effectively. For example, when discussing a drop in sales, a business owner should be able to explain the contributing factors (cause) and the resulting impact on the company (effect). Mastering this technique enables clear and logical presentation of ideas, making it easier for the audience to follow and understand the message.

Being adept at narrative—essentially, storytelling—is crucial for engaging and persuasive communication. Regardless of the technique being used, a compelling narrative can capture attention, build empathy, and convey complex ideas in an accessible way. For instance, when using the past-present-future structure, framing the information within a narrative context can make the progression more relatable and impactful. Similarly, in the problem-solution-benefits framework, telling a story about a specific challenge and how it was overcome can illustrate the benefits more vividly. A well-told story can transform abstract concepts into tangible experiences, making the message resonate more deeply with the audience.

Juxtaposition, the practice of placing contrasting ideas side by side, is a powerful tool for highlighting differences and making arguments more compelling. In communication, it involves presenting opposing viewpoints or scenarios to provide a more comprehensive understanding of the topic. For example, when discussing a strategic business decision, juxtaposing the potential risks against the expected benefits can provide a balanced view that aids in decision-making. This technique underscores the natural duality in life—much like matter and antimatter or synonyms and antonyms—and helps in presenting a well-rounded argument.

Now, let's explore the three main communication structures in detail. The past-present-future technique involves structuring your message by discussing the past, present, and future of a topic. It is particularly effective for expressing ideas clearly and chronologically. Begin by explaining the historical context (past), then describe the current situation (present), and finally outline the potential developments (future). For instance, when presenting a new business strategy, you could start by discussing past challenges and achievements, move on to current capabilities and resources, and conclude with future goals and projections. This structure provides a logical flow that helps the audience understand how past experiences shape the present and influence the future.

The what-so what-what now framework helps in making your message relevant and actionable. Start with stating the fact or situation (what), then explain its significance (so what), and finally suggest the next steps (what now). For example, if you're introducing a new product, you might start by describing the product features (what), explain why these features matter to the customer (so what), and then outline how the product can be used or purchased (what now). This technique ensures that your communication is not only informative but also drives the audience towards a clear course of action.

The problem-solution-benefits structure is ideal for addressing challenges and proposing effective solutions. Begin by clearly defining the problem, then present a viable solution, and finally, highlight the benefits of implementing this solution. For instance, when proposing a new marketing strategy, you could start by identifying the problem (declining customer engagement), propose a solution (a new social media campaign), and then outline the benefits (increased brand awareness and customer loyalty). This method ensures that your communication is focused on problem-solving and demonstrates the value of your proposed actions.

By mastering these communication structures and the foundational concepts of cause and effect, narrative, and juxtaposition, business owners and entrepreneurs can significantly enhance their communication skills. These techniques will not only be useful for regular communications but also serve as comprehensive rubrics for generating ideas faster and structuring them better. This, in turn, will improve business relationships and overall interactions, ensuring that your messages are clear, respectful, and impactful.

Integrating these insights and strategies will foster a culture of transparency, trust, and mutual respect within your business, paving the way for sustained success and growth. As we proceed, you will find that these techniques, combined with a deep understanding of the darker sides of communication, will equip you with the tools needed to navigate the complexities of business interactions effectively.

Innovation

Traditional methods are being reshaped by new technologies and a deeper understanding of global and digital dynamics. This book explores innovative strategies that can help both business owners and their enterprises thrive by integrating intuitive decision-making, global connectivity, brain science, historical trends, flexible work environments, and interdisciplinary insights. By adopting these approaches, businesses can remain competitive and adaptive in an ever-changing world.

Intuitive decision-making, combined with digital tools, represents a powerful approach to predicting market trends and making informed decisions. This method involves training leaders to leverage their gut instincts alongside digital analytics. By integrating intuition with data-driven insights, businesses can enhance their ability to foresee market shifts and consumer preferences. For instance, a tech company might use virtual reality simulations to predict consumer behavior, providing a valuable edge in product development and marketing. This blend of intuition and technology ensures that decisions are both innovative and grounded in reality.

Innovation and global connectivity are crucial for creating solutions that meet diverse market needs. Businesses must harness insights from various cultures to drive innovation and develop products that resonate globally. By tapping into the wealth of knowledge available from different regions, companies can create offerings that are not only innovative but also culturally relevant. For example, a multinational corporation might draw inspiration from multiple cultural insights to design products that cater to a wide range of consumer preferences, thereby expanding its global reach and impact.

Understanding how the environment affects the brain can significantly enhance creative thinking and problem-solving. By creating environments that stimulate the brain, businesses can foster a culture of innovation. For example, incorporating outdoor learning spaces in schools has been shown to boost student creativity. Similarly, businesses can design workspaces that encourage creative thinking by providing diverse and stimulating environments. This approach not only enhances employee well-being but also drives innovation and productivity within the organization.

Predicting the future by analyzing historical trends and current data is a powerful strategy for staying ahead of the curve. Businesses can use predictive analytics and artificial intelligence to forecast future opportunities and challenges. By examining past trends, companies can identify patterns and apply this knowledge to anticipate market shifts. For example, a company that foresaw the rise of remote work solutions before the pandemic was better positioned to adapt to the new normal. This foresight allowed them to develop and market products that met the emerging needs of remote workers, giving them a competitive advantage.

Supporting dynamic careers with flexible work arrangements is essential for attracting and retaining top talent. Modern work policies must accommodate diverse lifestyles and career paths, offering options for remote and flexible work. By embracing these arrangements, businesses can support their employees' work-life balance and improve overall job satisfaction. A company that effectively transitioned to a flexible work environment can serve as a model, demonstrating how such policies can enhance productivity and employee morale while maintaining operational efficiency.

Combining insights from different fields, such as psychology, technology, and sociology, can significantly improve business strategies and workplace environments. Interdisciplinary approaches allow businesses to draw from a broader range of knowledge and perspectives, leading to more holistic and effective solutions. For example, an urban development firm might use psychological research to design workspaces that enhance employee well-being and productivity. By integrating insights from various disciplines, businesses can create environments that are not only functional but also supportive of their employees' needs and goals.

By leveraging intuitive decision-making, global connectivity, brain science, historical trends, flexible work policies, and interdisciplinary approaches, business owners can create resilient and innovative organizations. These strategies not only enhance business performance but also contribute to a positive and supportive workplace culture, ensuring long-term success and growth.

Epilogue

ongratulations on embarking on this remarkable journey of business ownership and entrepreneurship. Your boldness and dedication have brought you this far, and now it's time to reflect on the core principles that will guide you towards enduring success. This journey has been about much more than just business; it's been about mastering the art of commerce and understanding the deeper principles that drive meaningful and sustainable growth.

Throughout this book, we have explored a multitude of ideas, methodologies, tips, tools, and perspectives. Each concept, whether it was about intention, core values, decision-making, or communication, was introduced not to give you all the answers, but to help you discover them for yourself. The true essence of learning and growth comes from staying curious, asking questions, and continuously seeking to understand more about yourself and your business.

My goal for this conclusion is not to re-explain every topic but to remind you of the importance of curiosity and exploration. These topics are indeed complex, and that's why it's crucial to keep an open mind and never stop asking questions. It's through this relentless pursuit of knowledge and understanding that you will find the answers you need and the inspiration to keep pushing forward.

In a world where distractions are plentiful and focus is a

fleeting commodity, it's easy to get lost in the noise and lose sight of what truly matters. But by maintaining a mindset of curiosity and intentionality, you can cut through the clutter and stay aligned with your vision and goals. This book has been crafted to help you navigate this path, offering insights that prompt you to think deeply and act purposefully.

Remember, the concepts of intuitive decision-making, global connectivity, innovation, and leadership we discussed are tools for you to adapt and integrate into your unique business context. They are not definitive answers but starting points for your journey. Use them to inspire your thinking, to challenge the status quo, and to drive your business forward with a sense of purpose and direction.

The essence of this book lies in its intent to empower you to think critically, to question assumptions, and to forge your own path. The principles of courage, integrity, and stewardship, along with effective communication and innovative strategies, are meant to be lenses through which you view your business and the world around you. They provide a framework but leave room for your creativity and individuality to shine.

As you continue on your entrepreneurial journey, let these insights guide you but also allow yourself the freedom to explore and experiment. The business landscape is ever-changing, and the ability to adapt and innovate is key to sustained success. Keep an open mind, stay curious, and never stop learning. Surround yourself with people who challenge you, who support your vision, and who bring diverse perspectives to the table.

Your journey is unique, and your business has its own story to tell. By embracing the principles discussed in this book, you are well-equipped to write that story with intention, purpose, and passion. Remember, the goal is not to have all the answers but to be willing to seek them out, to learn from every experience, and to continuously evolve.

I am genuinely excited about what you can achieve with your business. The potential is limitless, and the journey is filled with opportunities for growth and discovery. My hope is that this book has provided you with the tools and inspiration to pursue your vision with confidence and resilience. Keep asking questions, stay curious, and most importantly, believe in your ability to succeed. Our journey has just begun, and the best is yet to come!

Truth in simplicity, enlightenment in nature.

Joaby_Wan

www.ingramcontent.com/pod-product-compliance
Lightning Source LLC
Chambersburg PA
CBHW012054040426
42335CB00042B/2861